# I Got My Marbles Back
## There IS Life After Loss

Tonya Cunningham

To all who have suffered loss of any kind,
Seek to be healed physically, spiritually, emotionally, and behaviorally
Allow the Holy Spirit of God to infuse you as you do the work of
healing
May God be with you always

This book is also dedicated to the memory of
My baby – Chelsea Neashelle Adams
My mother – Willie Jean "Marie" Tippens Cunningham
My father – O.A. Cunningham
My mentor – Dr. Gregory W. Spencer
My former identity and dreams

# CONTENTS

# ACKNOWLEDGMENTS

Thank God for this opportunity to share my healing journey.

Thanks to my village (family and friends) for supporting me and loving me back to life. You know who you are.

Special thanks to my head villagers: my sisters, brother-in-love, nephews, nieces and cousin who is like a brother.
Thanks for always taking care of me.

Thank you to the Tonya Cunningham Ministries Support Team. There is no way I could fulfill this God-given vision without you guys. You always represent the Kingdom of God in excellence and humility.

Heartfelt thanks to my midwives who helped birth this book:
Glenda Garrity, Mildred Marshall, Zerita Hall, Donna Austin, Leigh Holland and Donna Kirvin
Lisa Bell – the best editor and writing coach on the planet. There is no way I could have completed this project without you. You are an angel from God.

# INTRODUCTION

*"The farther back you can look,*
*the farther forward you are likely to see."*
Winston Churchill

This book is my life map detailing events that contributed to the individual I am today. Life Mapping is a powerful tool used to help explore the many factors that shape who you are from childhood to the present. Each chapter is designed for you to see yourself through the eyes of my story. For you see, everybody has a story. Behind every face, an untold story lies hidden, sometimes even from the story's owner.

I am a firm believer in healing from storytelling. When

we share our stories, the light shines on our hearts and somehow the process soothes the deepest of wounds. As we tell our stories, opportunities for personal growth and stress reduction blossom. And in the process, those listening catch some of the balm working in our hearts. Ps 107:2 says, "All of you set free by God, tell the world! Tell how he freed you from oppression." (The Message Bible)

Of course, we must use wisdom in how and when we tell our stories. Some people don't understand or maybe they aren't quite ready to listen. But overall, I encourage each of you to allow yourself to walk down the corridors of your mind. Uncover those painful places, losses, and life transitions you buried, and no one knows about. As you walk, some moments hurt more than others do.

Be of good courage. Enduring the pain for a moment brings intense joy at the end of the road.

On this journey, you will discover the pivotal moments that happened to you and/or influenced important decisions you made.

Pain, fear, depression, divorce, instability, lack—these are just a few life experiences that plague our lives. Good news. No matter what you've been through or are currently going through, God can take those painful chapters of your life and bring you to a place of restoration and peace. For all things work together for your good, according to the Word of God. It doesn't matter how your story started.

With God, you are guaranteed to win.

"'This Temple is going to end up far better than it started out, a glorious beginning but an even more glorious finish: a place in which I will hand out wholeness and holiness.' Decree of God-of-the-Angel-Armies." Haggai 2:9 (The Message Bible)

While every individual's journey is unique, I pray that through my journey, God will reveal to you the unspoken hurts that hinder you from being whole. I hope you will find the courage to tell your own story, so the healing can begin.

Peace and love to you,

Tonya Cunningham, LBSW, MA

# CHAPTER 1
# WAITING TO EXHALE

Like most little girls, I grew up watching fairy tales, believing in happily ever after. But living in a fantasy world doesn't last. Harsh reality breaks in stealing all hope of a prince riding in on his white horse to rescue us from life. We wait for a knight, complete with shining armor, but in our naivety, we settle for a jerk wearing a dented trash can, while convincing ourselves he is perfect.

The 1995 film *Waiting to Exhale*[1], adapted from Terry McMillian's 1992 novel, focuses on four friends - Savannah, Robin, Bernadine, and Gloria - and their relationships with men as well as each other. Each woman comes from a different background. All of them hold their breath until the day they can exhale and feel comfortable in

[1] (Edmonds, 1995)

a committed relationship with a man. The bond of their friendship becomes stronger as men, families, and careers take them down separate paths. While processing through problems and struggles with love and life, they provide emotional support for one another.

Savannah, a successful television producer and mistress, holds on to hope that one day her married lover will leave his wife for her. In the meantime, she looks for temporary relationships, using her beauty to draw men.

Robin is a high-powered executive and the long-time mistress of a married man as well. She clings to hope of his promise to leave his wife no matter what he does or says. He always puts his wife above her needs. Even while hanging to hope, she seeks someone to fill the void and love her above everyone else.

As most wives do, Bernadine abandons her own career aspirations and dreams of owning a catering business to raise a family and support her husband and his dreams. He leaves her for another woman—a white woman, which in her mind makes his indiscretion and betrayal worse.

And lastly, Gloria, the long-term single mother of the group, owns a beauty salon. Years of emotional abuse and rejection from her son's father rips her self-esteem to shreds. She blames his rejection on her weight gain. Later, he confesses to her—he is gay. The feeble attempt at explaining why he tossed her aside fails to raise her self-worth.

In all four cases, the friends have two things in common; bad relationships with men, based on belief they found the perfect one, and a deep loss of self-respect. To varying degrees, all of these characters accepted brutalization of their emotions.

I am no stranger to emotional abuse. In my late 20's as a single woman, I secretly suffered both emotional and physical abuse at the hands of an angry man—abuse hidden behind invisible scars, yet equally as devastating.

We dated for several years. From the onset, emotional abuse entered the relationship. He was very dominant, controlling my every move. He isolated me from family and friends. As he pummeled my heart and mind with his words, behavior and attitude, I had no support system—no one to speak truth. I believed the man's lies.

Then one day, he hit me. I don't remember why. The emotional abuse escalated to violence. Blood spewed from my nose. I fell to the floor like a cannon ball, hitting hard. His foot stomped my thigh, leaving a big shoe print. The one-time event left these and other war wounds etched in my memory forever.

I lay on the floor, heaviness pressing down over my body and thought to myself, "What in the world are you doing, girl? You deserve better than this!" And after years of meanness, I almost believed my own words—almost.

I knew the relationship was unhealthy, and I needed to get out of it, but I didn't know how. At the time, I didn't realize I had become a victim of domestic abuse. Using such a harsh phrase doesn't come easily. Using such a harsh word compels a woman to take action. And using such a harsh description of my perfect relationship wasn't an option.

He bruised my soul, the seat of my emotions and center of my human personality. I thought if I left him, I wouldn't find another man to love me. The effects of abuse were devastating, crippling me of identity and self-worth.

Since I couldn't get myself out of the bad relationship, I sought help from a counselor. Me—a strong, independent, educated woman needed someone to save me. For the very first time in my life, I pursued help. Maybe because deep down in the depth of my soul I felt my life depended on it.

So the day finally arrived for my first counseling session.

I must admit, initially, I was NOT impressed with the counselor. From my limited knowledge base of counseling at that time, he just sat there with a tablet and pen, nodding his head in support of me while listening to me talk, cry, rant and rave.

How could this counselor who did and said nothing lead my life to healing? I didn't feel any better. Nothing changed.

Then one day during a session, the light bulb came on, I got an epiphany, a revelation, whatever you want to name it.

Tears tumbled, creating a broken path down my cheeks. "All I want him to do is love me. Is that too much to ask for?"

My counselor leaned forward, and the life changing response spurted from his mouth. "Stop expecting him to do what he CANNOT do. He DOES love you but it's the way HE knows how to love. Remember, he came from a dysfunctional home, and he gave you the love he received."

The counselor helped me realize I sought love from a man, while I did not love myself. I expected him to do what I could not even do—love me.

As if someone literally cut a switch on in my mind, I

immediately understood what the counselor said. There was an abrupt transformation of my mind.

I went home and applied the principle of no expectations of love my way. The loving myself came gradually, but circumstances changed at once.

Perhaps my boyfriend recognized a change in my mindset or the way I interacted with him. He began to do and say all the things I wanted him to do prior to the abuse. He only hit me that one time, but now, it was too late. I made my exodus in my mind first, long before my epiphany. After I received that illumination, I completed the physical exodus.

It's important to realize that none of us is exempt from life experiences. Even though I am a social worker and should have known better, I found myself in a no-win relationship and needed professional help to leave.

Simple relationship principle—I don't demand love my way, expecting others to treat me in a way they can't, especially if I don't love myself. I have shared the principle with others and applied it to every relationship—and it works!

From a spiritual standpoint, God told me not to get in the relationship, but because of my disobedience to God and my insecurities, I settled for a man who disrespected me. As a result of that poor decision, I almost lost my life to abuse. A piece of me died, along with the relationship and fantasy of happily-ever-after. These internal deaths smothered me with grief as strong as any physical experience I ever knew.

You see, I was like Savannah in *Waiting to Exhale*. I pretended this man was everything I ever dreamed of and that he was the one I waited for all my life. He loved me, and some day, what we shared would be perfect.

I was waiting to exhale.

## Scripture: Proverbs 11:14 NKJV

*"Where there is no counsel, the people fall; but in the multitude of counselors, there is safety."*

## Grief Nugget:

*"All losses must be mourned, even if they are unhealthy relationships."*

*~Tonya Cunningham, LBSW, MA*

## Self-Reflection:

What abuse have you endured during your lifetime? (Physical, emotional, verbal, sexual, financial)

Have you mourned the losses resulting from the abuse? (Sexuality, childhood, identity, loved one, home, etc.)

# CHAPTER 2
# A LOVE WORTH WAITING FOR

Once upon a time, there was a girl called Cinderella, her real name lost in circumstances of life. Her father, a widower, remarried, choosing a woman who kept her dark side hidden from him. The wicked stepmother had two daughters, equally evil and selfish. The father often traveled on business, taking trips that lasted for extended periods. All three of the new family members continually abused and forced Cinderella into servitude.

Her day began before the sun rose and continued late into the evening. Each day, after working for her stepmother and stepsisters, Cinderella retired to her bleak, cold room and curled up near the fireplace in an effort to stay warm during the long winter nights. She often woke covered in cinders from the fireplace, thus intensifying the mockery of her nickname.

Although she didn't doubt her father's love, she feared he wouldn't believe her if she mentioned the abuse. Like most teenage children, she thought he would take his wife's side against her.

Then one day, the father died. And the abuse grew, with the evil stepmother taking away all privileges. The stepsisters pilfered her best clothes, leaving only the most ragged for the young girl.

So Cinderella began to live life through her dreams.

One day she heard that the beloved Prince Charming was hosting a ball—a spectacular event specifically designed to choose a wife from the attendees. Dreaming and wishing she could attend the grand event with her stepsisters, Cinderella cried in despair. All of a sudden, her Fairy Godmother appeared and granted the wish. Without explanation, Cinderella suddenly transformed from an ordinary girl to a beautiful princess. Although she stepped into her dream, she quickly realized the magic had a catch. Kind of like a 'b' clause on a document or a disclaimer listed in fine print at the bottom of a page.

Fairy Godmother said, "Cinderella, have a blast. But you must leave the ball before midnight or otherwise be exposed as a commoner."

The voice of Fairy Godmother reverberated throughout Cinderella's empty, lifeless room with a fresh gust of hope. "Oh I will, I will. Thank you."

"The spell will be broken at midnight. Make haste and get back home."

Like every girl there, Cinderella enjoyed the ball. Fully enchanted by the prince, she lost track of time. The clock chimed, one…two…three. Reality burst in her brain and with urgency, she fled the ball as the stroke of midnight came, leaving one of her glass slippers on the stairwell.

The prince, deeply infatuated with Cinderella, chased after her when she abruptly departed. He retrieved the glass slipper, vowing to find and marry the beautiful owner. The prince tried the glass slipper on all of the women in the kingdom. Girls lined up for miles to try on the slipper in hopes of being the lucky one to become his bride even though they knew it didn't belong to them. Finally, he got to Cinderella and naturally, the shoe fit her perfectly. Cinderella married Prince Charming, and they live happily ever after—so we are told.

This fairytale story remains popular and continues to influence numerous cultures throughout the world. Most every little girl dreams of marrying Prince Charming (or a true-life version of him) and having an elegant storybook wedding.

I must admit that as a young girl, I secretly dreamed of one day marrying Prince Charming and riding off while pastel sunset colors dripped favor on us.

Even though faced with pressure from society to get married because my internal clock was ticking, I didn't buckle under the intimidation from others to jump into marriage just to experience the wedding day in a beautiful white gown. With confidence, I combatted the questions, "Why are you still single? You don't want to be an old maid, do you?"

I waited late in life to marry my prince charming. I remained in readiness, preparing for the purposes of marriage by becoming a confident, self-sufficient, single woman.

Our story held the awe of a fairytale as well. Neither of us had been married before. We were strong people of faith, solid in our conviction of God's sovereignty. For several years, we served well alongside each other in a local church when out of nowhere, something changed for me.

I secretly started liking him.

I wouldn't dare express my feelings. He was not the knight in shining armor I dreamed about since childhood. And neither was I the young whippersnapper bride, waiting for him.

One day I drove down I30. As I passed Six Flags, an overwhelming desire poured over me. I hadn't gone there since high school. That day, in my late 30's, I wanted to be a kid again, soaring on rides, eating junk and having fun. I didn't have much money, so I dismissed it, not divulging the secret desire to anyone.

Then shortly after that day, my prince called. "Do you want to go to Six Flags with me?"

I didn't hesitate. Free meal ticket to do something I wanted. Calming my voice, I said, "Yes. That sounds fun."

My heart beat faster than a roller coaster as thoughts raced through my mind. Was this a date? No one knew I liked him—no one. Except God. I held a breath wedged in my throat, afraid to release it, and equally afraid to hope. I didn't dare exhale.

The day arrived. He invited another couple to go with us, a double date. But it felt somewhat like chaperones, creating a romantic glow to the day. We rode in their car. I pushed aside expectations for the day, convincing myself God was in control of whatever happened. I still breathed lightly.

By the time we reached the parking lot, I was ready to jump out of the car and go have fun.

Instead, my prince paused and pulled out a little black box. "Will you be my queen for the Kingdom of God?"

A moment of shock passed, my heart standing still for a second. "Yes," I screamed and then leaped out of the car into his arms.

Our friends applauded and congratulated both of us. During the day, I learned they knew about the proposal. He went to them and our spiritual father for advice about proposing to me. He felt led by God to marry me. After receiving wise counsel, he took an unusual path. Because of what we perceived as the leading of the Holy Spirit, we got engaged and then started dating. The exact opposite of what society dictates for marriage, but the road we chose together.

Everyone thought we made the ideal couple—or if they didn't they kept their objections silent. Two spiritual powerhouses, coming together as one. I couldn't understand WHY I was attracted to him.

I said to myself, "This has to be the Holy Spirit because we are totally opposite in every physical way possible."

I believed this was God's purpose and plan for my life, based entirely on what seemed to be a leading of the Holy Spirit. I said 'yes to the dress.' And like almost every blushing bride-to-be, the planning began.

We chose the theme, A Love Worth Waiting For. June 28, 2003 arrived—the day I married my prince charming. It was all I anticipated the day could be with the one I loved.

A picturesque' event, filled with all the joys and stresses a wedding day can bring. A beautiful young harpist greeted our guests in the foyer with angelic music, calming the atmosphere.

Hundreds of people filled the majestic sanctuary of the church to capacity, there to witness our nuptials and either share in our joy or simply spectate. The long aisle stretched down the middle of the room. Fresh cut flowers released a gentle scent, and stain-glassed windows filtered sunlight through the windows. They all joined with other amenities, creating a beautiful aroma of worship. In my mind, the perfect backdrop for a majestic wedding.

The moment I awaited all my life finally arrived—time

for me to walk down the aisle into the arms of my prince.

*The doors to the sanctuary remain closed as I wait to make my grand entrance into the sanctuary. I hear nothing but silence. Oh the magnitude of the silence! My heart palpitates, what feels like a thousand beats a minute. Hair and make-up flawless, elegant wedding gown on fleek. All of the pieces to the puzzle appear accounted for. The doors slowly open, giving me one last opportunity to gaze into the eyes of my father, thinking "I'm about to marry a man like you Daddy. A man who will love me and protect me like you have for 38 years." I smile, and take the first step down the aisle as the hand-bell choir plays the traditional bridal march.*

*"Here Comes the Bride" resounds through the massive space, bouncing back from the wall and filling me with even greater anticipation.*

*Yes, here I come.*

Finally, I exhaled.

## Scripture: Amos 3:3 The Message Bible

*"Do two people walk hand in hand if they aren't going to the same place?"*

## Grief nugget:

*"When you lose love, you grieve."*

*~Tonya Cunningham, LBSW, MA*

## Self-Reflection:

Were your parents positive or negative role models in displaying love?

How do you define love?

Do you know what your love language is? If not, read *The Five Love Languages: How to Express Heartfelt Commitment to Your Mate* by Gary Chapman

# CHAPTER 3
## WHEN TRAGEDY COMES

Growing up as a child, I often heard my mother say, "If you keep living, you will find yourself in a storm, just coming out of a storm or headed into a storm."

Of course, I didn't give credence to her then, but having lived and matured for a half-century, I've accepted that statement as true. Life happens to all of us. Generally, we live our lives in a world marked by assumptions. We wake up in the morning and assume life will be much as it was yesterday. But when tragedy or loss happens to us or someone we care about, our world of assumption is threatened, if not shattered. We then must face this unknown phenomenon called "grief."

The previous chapter exudes the happiness I experienced on my wedding day. I finally got the opportunity to marry my prince charming. When I exhaled, years of waiting and wondering ended—blown out from a place deep in my soul.

In reality, my wedding day dawned bittersweet. Yes, I married the man of my dreams, overjoyed at the sweetness and beauty of our special day. But only three days prior to the wedding my funeral service mentor's untimely death rocked my world, leaving a deep wake of sadness. Tragedy marched its way into my life, altering it forever.

How could I feel bliss in the crashing waves of sorrow?

My mentor's death traumatized me in major ways. I missed his friendship, but he was also my wedding coordinator, a jack-of-all-trades. The sorrow of his death stung, but the fear of a less than perfect wedding screamed at me.

On Monday, the week of the wedding, I stopped by the funeral home to visit with my mentor.

"Is there anything else I need to do for the wedding?" As a blushing bride, anytime I thought of my wedding day, my nerves bristled, accelerating my pulse as if I'd been running.

He stated, "Everything is perfect. I have it all under control. Just show up at the church on Saturday and be beautiful. It will be a day you will NEVER forget!"

My mentor chose to keep all wedding day plans a secret. His wedding gift to me was coordination of the wedding day, which included making floral arrangements, printing of programs, and providing transportation for the wedding party. I had no reason to doubt his abilities.

Wednesday came, a vivid memory I carry with me.

One of the few tasks I owned, the final fitting of my gown, required time at the bridal store. Before I headed out that morning, I received a call from an acquaintance.

A probing voice came over the phone. "Have you heard from Dr. Spencer today?"

"Not since last night when I was at the funeral home. Why do you ask?"

The answer rattled me. "Rumor has it that he's missing. Gotta go." Instant silence filled my ear.

"Hello?" No answer. I took a deep breath, calming myself. "I saw him yesterday. He was fine," I said to the empty room.

I rushed off to the bridal store, assuring my girlfriend and myself. "Everything is perfect. And it can't be perfect if he is missing. He's attending to wedding details, that's all."

Standing in the bridal store, I looked in the mirror,

twirling to see the dress and check the way it fit me. Perfect. My heart soared. Only three more days.

My girlfriend watched, smiling. "You're so beautiful, Tonya."

"Really?"

"Amazing." Her phone chirped cutting the admiration of my beauty short.

The countenance on her face dropped. My mind rushed back to the call I received that morning. I immediately knew the rumor was true.

She clicked off the phone. "Sit down."

I didn't sit. "They found him didn't they?"

"Yes, honey. He's… He's dead, Tonya."

My mentor and my wedding planner—dead. I screamed, a piercing cry searching for comfort. Dead? Missing, okay. But dead? It couldn't be true. I started running around the dressing room in despair. I couldn't breathe. I couldn't think. A million thoughts rushed through my mind like a tsunami, hitting all at once, drowning me.

My fiancé and girlfriend calmed me down and we headed to the funeral home. Mass pandemonium hung in the atmosphere, cars parked absolutely everywhere. I quickly realized I wasn't the only one dealing with disbelief.

We wanted answers. What happened to him? Why was he snatched away from us?

Local pastors and community leaders attempted to gain control of the massive crowd and provide support to the community as well as the funeral home staff. After spending time with my funeral service colleagues, my fiancé and I left the funeral home. We couldn't do anything else at that point.

We went to my parents' home to debrief with family and determine what we would do about the wedding logistics that died along with my mentor. We found so many people present at my parents' house that it appeared they all followed us from the funeral home. People walking up and down the street in disbelief, phones ringing continuously, extreme devastation.

The cause of death brought another wave of shock. Why would someone murder this wonderful man? None of it made sense. The brutal reality clung to me, my emotions sticking in my throat, constricting until I dared not speak.

Should I postpone the wedding? My mentor would say no. People from the community came to our rescue in donating their services and executing wedding logistics. The flowers, programs and cars were all in place within three days. So we moved forward in spite of our grief.

My mentor was right. I showed up at the church on Saturday, stunning in my wedding gown. It was a day I will never forget—amazing and perfect except for his absence. The brutal murder thrust a shadow of sorrow everywhere, tainting the joyous occasion.

From the moment we said, "I do," life already raced out of control, building tension in the relationship. My time-off canceled, we didn't get to take our honeymoon. My mentoring time ended abruptly, and they thrust me into funeral director mode, serving in any capacity needed. From picking up trash on the parking lot to making funeral arrangements for other families experiencing tragedy in their lives as well. No time to grieve, I pushed forward, comforting others while my own heart blistered from pain.

My husband and I mustered up enough strength to navigate through that stressful and painful inception of a marriage. Not long after our marriage, God blessed us with new life—a precious baby girl we planned to greet in February. Mourning switched to joy, my sorrow became dancing. I visited my OB/GYN early in October and received a clean bill of health. Everything was perfect. On target for a February 2005 birth.

A couple of days later on a Thursday night, I stood before the women's group at our church, teaching. All of a sudden, the room blurred. Words coming from my mouth and spoken by others entered my mind muffled. As quick as the light-headedness came, it departed. A very strange episode, but it passed quickly. I hadn't experienced any problems with the pregnancy, other than the typical nausea symptoms. Nonetheless, the episode startled the women, so they forced me to sit down since I demanded to keep teaching. I felt better—no reason to stop.

At the end of our women's meeting, we gathered in a circle to pray. I felt led to sing an old hymn entitled, "Fix me Jesus." Of course, we pastored a younger generation, and they did not know the words to the hymn. Their expressions indicated that they thought I was crazy for singing it. But I kept singing it until I felt released to stop.

On October 8, 2004, we faced yet another tragedy, this one more powerful than any pain imaginable. My sweet angel, Chelsea, flew into my life and made her departure within a span of 2 hours and 12 minutes. Without warning, she came and then left.

My heart ripped apart. I knew grief—felt it so deeply just over a year earlier with my mentor. But this—I couldn't understand this death. Incomprehensible. A violation of the natural order of life. Chelsea was supposed to bury me. I was supposed to die long before she did, leaving her standing beside my grave, weeping. Not the other way around.

Any death is difficult to accept and cope with, but the death of a child—my child—inexplicable. Everything was perfect—but life changed, leaving the most traumatic moment imaginable crashing over me. Why did this happen? My perfect pregnancy wrenched from me before my time, with no explanation.

Death shows no discrimination. It crosses all cultural and socioeconomic boundaries. A child's death can be one of the most traumatic events a family can experience, leaving them with gaping wounds, each heart ripped to different degrees, and creating tension and conflict.

The belief that parents can push past the death of a child quicker because they have each other is not so. Both mother and father must bear their own pain of grief. Of course, it holds true that men and women experience grief differently. Women tend to grieve more deeply for longer periods while men tend to focus more on tasks than relationship. Their grief becomes unobservable due to the social mores stating men don't cry.

This held true for my marriage. I allowed grief to paralyze me to the point of not wanting to conceive again. I never, ever want to experience that excruciating pain of losing a child to death again. Never.

I know many women have miscarriages and later on have successful pregnancies. God bless them! As for me, I couldn't do it. It was too much for me to bear again.

As I grieved, I cried out to the Lord. I still couldn't comprehend the reasons for her death. After a series of losses, I understand why she is with God in Heaven instead of with me on earth. For that revelation, I am grateful to God.

Hindsight is 20/20. Months later, I looked back to that Thursday night when I experienced the strange light-headedness. I didn't understand the purpose of the hymn that night—why I chose the particular one and kept singing. My baby was about to be born and die the very next day. And even though I didn't know, God did. In His own way, He prepared me for what was coming.

Before long, my husband thrust himself into building a relationship with a troubled young boy from the church. Shortly after our baby died, we took him into our home in an effort to help him.

Yet another loss for me. You may be thinking, "How can helping a young boy experiencing difficulties in life be a loss for someone else?" I'm so glad you asked me to explain.

First of all, bringing this boy into our home was something my husband wanted to do. Because I loved and supported him, I agreed to allow the move in, with hopes of being a positive influence in the teen's life. Looking back and assessing the situation, allowing the young boy into our home was the beginning of the demise of our marriage.

From my perspective, it felt like I lost a piece of my husband because he gave more of himself to the church and the young boy than to me and our marriage. After all, we were still newlyweds married in June 2003, pastoring a new church in September 2003, and coping with the death of our baby in October 2004. So much in a little time period.

But life pushed on. Two years later in June 2006, my mother made her transition to be with the Lord.

I faced extreme difficulty when my mother left this earth. I already struggled with my identity as a mother since the only child birthed through my loins died. Now, my maternal influence gone, I desperately needed some lady to mother me and help me through this challenging time in life. My sisters were great support, but they lost their mother too, so I didn't share my needs with them. The pain in my heart expanded. Lost and alone, I didn't know how to process yet another loss.

A dear friend and colleague in the grief industry, and now mentor reached out to me. She helped me understand that I am a mother even though my daughter died. She also provided the motherly guidance I so desperately needed back then. My mother died just a few days before a milestone birthday celebration for my husband. I coordinated his birthday celebration while she was dying.

After the death of my mother, my husband realized my father needed help through his grief process. He was like a fish out of water without my mother.

He said, "We are going to have to move in with your father to help him." I immediately dispelled that idea because, at the time, I perceived moving back to my childhood home as a demotion. I was working hard to move forward in life and now to go backwards was not good for me. Wasn't losing my mother enough of a loss? Yet I stood at a crossroads, grieving a secondary loss of my independence. Even worse, how would this move affect our life as a married couple?

I bit the bullet and consented to moving back home to care for my father, and I'm so glad we did. That time afforded me precious memories with him I would not otherwise have. Nevertheless, it added another layer of sorrow to an already tender place.

So, our young family—my husband, the troubled teenage boy and me—moved in with my father.

Shortly after the move, my husband said, "I want to adopt a son—legally this time."

A part of me resisted because I lost so much of my husband when the teen moved in. But again, because I loved him, I opened myself to adopting a kid. I gave all of me, as much as my husband allowed, to those boys as if they came from my own loins. At the time, my husband allowed me to stay at home, caring for my father and the boys, and fulfilling church administrative duties.

We entered the adoption process, with a ton of paperwork and countless meetings, evaluations, home visits and many other tasks to complete. The stress compounded, creating even more strain on our marriage. But we survived, building memories with my father. We completed the adoption. I became a mother, a full time job by itself, taking care of two sons—one legally adopted, the other not. We quickly grew from a family of three to a family of four. An overabundance of testosterone filled the atmosphere of our home, but our blended family was not so blended.

Still, surely the worst trauma lay behind us. We already endured so much. Grief set aside, life pressed forward.

Then in August 2009, on the Friday night of my 25th year high school class reunion, I enjoyed the event, connecting with old friends. In spite of my years of trauma, I finished the evening with a thankful heart and fresh perspective. Some of my schoolmates had wonderful lives, others mediocre and very similar to mine. A few went through even worse times than I experienced.

I arrived home after the reunion to find out the troubled teenage boy we took in left our home. I didn't know how to feel, why he left. Everything seemed good. The kid simply disappeared.

"Did he give you any reasons for leaving?" I asked my husband.

He shrugged his shoulders and shook his head. "No idea."

He wasn't legally our son, so we couldn't do much about his leaving. I cared about him and wondered what drove him away from our home. I had no idea where he went, but hoped the best for him. Maybe he made amends with his mother and returned home.

Then on Sunday, a snowball of tragedy fell and intensified, becoming an unstoppable avalanche that threatened to bury me.

My husband walked into our bedroom. "I have to tell you something. About the kid…"

I waited patiently. He looked away. "What about him?" I asked.

"He accused me of sexual abuse."

My heart sank to the floor like a ton of bricks, imploding with a loud crash in my brain. Never in my life had I been involved in anything to this magnitude. Speechless, I reached for my husband. He turned and left the room. Yet again, I lost another piece of my husband to the madness surrounding this little boy.

Over the next days and weeks, I attempted to support and reach out to my husband. But a chasm as big as the Grand Canyon rose between us kept getting wider and wider every day. To the public eye, we appeared to be the power couple standing strong together, when in reality all hell was breaking loose in our lives.

For months, we endured the embarrassment of this exposure, both of us maintaining his innocence. Why would this young boy make such crazy allegations? Because he was a teacher, the school district suspended my husband's job. At the same time, we shelled out attorney fees. Questioning eyes watched us. Could he have done such a thing? And if so, did I know and how could I not?

I stood faithfully by him, never asking if he did anything. Of course, this wasn't true. I couldn't imagine him molesting a child—especially not a boy. Yet my emotions tumbled, fighting the way out of this mountainous incident.

After a thorough investigation by the local authorities, they couldn't substantiate the accusations against my husband and dropped all charges. His name was cleared and restored. I thanked God for His goodness, seeing the entire incident as a test we overcame. He returned to work as a schoolteacher. I kept praying God would use my attitude during this devastating time to restore our marriage. But the hard times kept coming.

The year 2010 arrived, and my father made his transition to be with the Lord in June. My gentle giant, my hero, advocate, provider, and protector—gone. Alzheimer's disease slowly stole him away, but then cancer came along and took him from us without much warning. The patriarch of the Cunningham Family was no longer present to provide that fatherly touch and guidance.

I was indeed a daddy's girl. His death buried me under a bigger avalanche of sorrow, so deep I could never climb out of it. Still silently dealing with the residual effects of the sexual abuse allegations of my husband, I wasn't sure I wanted out. But I walked on, going through the motions and putting on the face of a happy wife, in partnership with a wonderful husband. On the surface, we still looked like a powerhouse couple able to face anything with grace.

I stood on that reputation and rested in the comfort of others seeing us that way. Two years later, my familiar little world, exploded into a million pieces.

February 24, 2012, my husband announced, "I no longer have the capacity to be married to you any longer."

"What? After all we went through?" After I stood by his side during every trial we faced? How could this be happening? I couldn't take anymore.

He no longer wanted me, and I no longer had the capacity to fight for our marriage. We parted.

For a long time after our separation, I struggled with understanding his reason. I get it now. He was right—he didn't have the capacity to be married to me.

One question reverberated through my mind more than any other did. I sent a text message to my husband. "How could God let me down like this?"

He replied, "God didn't let you down, I did."

I began to understand to a greater degree that it takes both people to maintain a relationship but only one to destroy or give up on it. He chose to end the marriage. I consented and simply put in action his desires and later filed for divorce, giving us both the freedom to do and become all God purposed for our individual lives.

When tragedy comes, it brings an awareness of life. Our perspective changes, and we view life through a different lens. Tragedy forces us to recognize the things we take for granted as well as affords us opportunities to increase our sensitivity in what we do and how we care for others.

I experienced so much over less than one decade. Is there anything to gain from tragedy and loss? Can I make sense of the pain?

Absolutely.

However, we cannot perceive what we gained unless we

are willing to process through the suffering of tragedy and release ourselves into the grip of grief.

## Scripture: Isaiah 43:2 The Message Bible

*"When you're in over your head, I'll be there with you. When you're in rough waters, you will not go down. When you're between a rock and a hard place, it won't be a dead end."*

## Grief nugget:

*"You must feel the pain in order to heal the pain."*

~Tonya Cunningham, LBSW, MA

## Self-Reflection:

What tragedies have you endured during your lifetime? Assess feelings felt when it happened versus today.

# CHAPTER 4
## THE SCARLET LETTER OF GRIEF

At a tender young age, a book entitled *The Scarlet Letter*[2] by Nathaniel Hawthorne captivated my attention. How could people treat a woman with such cruelty?

The book tells the story of a young woman named Hester Prynne who the judge found guilty of adultery. He requires her to wear a scarlet "A" (standing for adulterer) on her dress to bring shame. The book begins with guards leading Hester from the town prison to the scaffold in the middle of town. There she must stand for hours, exposed to public humiliation. A crowd of church folk gathers to witness her humiliation.

Throughout the book, the author examines themes of legalism, sin, and guilt, which are all terms that remind me

[2] (Hawthorne, 1850)

of the church today, and my experience of divorce from a pastor. Even though the book is a historical work of fiction, it speaks the sentiments of my heart today regarding my life experiences.

I wasn't an adulterer, but as I went through this heart-wrenching time of life, I felt as if I sinned. No one knew our circumstances.

After realizing the inevitable, that apparently we could not coexist, the planning to live separate lives began and lasted until the divorce was final. I didn't want any of this, but to live in a house where my husband had already emotionally checked out of the marriage caused more pain than my shattered heart could handle.

When the separation became reality, I immediately felt like the character Hester Prynne, rejected and abandoned because I knew we were headed to Judge Lynn Toler's divorce court. I hadn't ever experienced anything like it before, so I didn't know what to do or how to act. I guess I should've paid attention to the behavior of countless people who got divorced before me. Then again, I never imagined walking in their footsteps. I never imagined losing my dream. And I certainly never imagined falling into a state of depression.

During that time, I walked up to total strangers and introduced myself. "Hi, I'm Tonya Cunningham, and I'm divorced."

My bizarre behavior speaks of the eruption inside of me, like hot lava from a volcano. I literally felt like I wore the scarlet letter "D" which stood for domestic violence, divorce, and depression. On the outside, it looked as if everything was fine, but on the inside, a slow death ate away, leading toward total demise of my spirit. And no one knew it. I became a lifetime member of this country club called grief, divorce, or depression. I did not submit an application for membership, nor did I want it.

Nevertheless, I was in this exclusive club, separated from friends and family who didn't share affiliation with the club. Non-members don't get how you feel and why you react the way you do.

I started viewing others from my "Members Only" lenses before I shared my heart with them. If you haven't had any loss, hurt or pain in your life, I'm not accepting applications because you can't identify with my heart right now. That attitude became my familiar ground, my go to place for protecting the remains of my fractured soul.

Announcing my divorce to others gave me a feeble

attempt at easing the pain. I couldn't wrap my mind around what was happening to me. My life spiraled downward, and I couldn't stop it. I saw everything, but like having an out of body experience, I watched from far away. At the same time, I felt like everybody else already knew what was going on. I wanted to say let's just cut to the chase and get it over with.

An overwhelming sense of grief and betrayal consumed me to the point I couldn't sleep nor eat. I dropped 25 pounds in a month, and then I started hearing rumors that I was sick. I wasn't physically sick, but my emotions needed extreme healing.

My soul had been murdered leaving me grief stricken.

As a mortician and hospice social worker/bereavement coordinator, I learned a lot about grief over the years. I came to realize that grief is something everyone will experience at one point or another in life. When someone experiences the loss of someone he or she loves, through either death or divorce, that person faces grief. The individual chooses whether he or she deals with that grief. We must pay the grief "toll." We determine if we make that payment at the beginning of the loss, during, or at the end. Nonetheless, enduring loss demands a price—and one way or another we pay.

Because of my training and position, I knew about grief. From personal experience, I understood the price of pain arising from the ashes of loss.

I recognized in the onset of my life falling apart after the marriage that it's important to heal your heart after grief. Why? Because when you love and loose, you grieve. Nothing will change the loss that catapulted you to this new place in life. Grief is a process rather than a destination. Therefore, you must give yourself time to adjust to this new life journey. In order to get to the other side of grief, one must be willing to travel through the long corridor of pain to the peaceful place of solace and rest.

Grief is a natural, emotional response to ANY loss and must be experienced physically, spiritually, emotionally, and behaviorally. The internal nature of grief comes from a myriad of losses. We expect it from death, but divorce, loss of employment, a house, car, identity, and independence, just to name a few, also drop grief on us.

Grief has a way of marching into our lives and altering it forever. No one can change the reality of death and loss; however, we can change the way we respond when it occurs. Unfortunately, there are no easy answers. We can't always understand the 'why' of loss, but we always feel the impact of it.

Then, this grief phenomenon hits us square in the face with relentless force.

Dealing with grief requires work, and you must be willing to 'do grief work' in order to heal. The process allows you to feel the 'weight' of grief, making room for you to peel back the layers of hurt and pain to set the stage for your new life.

Peel back the layers of hurt, disappointment, guilt, shame, fear, rejection, abandonment, and anger in removing the Scarlet Letter D from your life.

At times, we simply want to move on in life, stuff the grief in a distant corner and move on with life. Ignore all of the layers as if they don't exist—but they do. We lug the grief with us, and it grows heavier and heavier, until finally, something breaks, and we have no choice but to look at the depths of grief and results of leaving it hidden.

"Grief never ends… But it changes. It's a passage, not a place to stay. Grief is not a sign of weakness, nor a lack of faith… It is the price of love." — Unknown

## Scripture: Isa 53:3 NKJV

*"He is despised and rejected by men, A Man of sorrows and acquainted with grief. And we hid, as it were, our faces from Him; He was despised, and we did not esteem Him."*

## Grief nugget:

*"Do your grief work."*

~ Tonya Cunningham, LBSW, MA

## Self-Reflection:

What life events have caused you to experience hurt, disappointment, guilt, shame, fear, rejection, abandonment, or anger?

What did you do to resolve those feelings?

# CHAPTER 5
## THE INVISIBLE ILLNESS

What you can't see does hurt you. Therefore, it's important to give attention to how your body, mind, and soul respond when life throws you a curve ball.

The average person is ok with going to the doctor to get a checkup on their body from head to toe. But we neglect to get a checkup from the neck up, especially when the exam has nothing to do with our physical beings. When we fracture a limb, we feel safe going to the doctor and getting a cast to support the healing process.

But when circumstances fracture our mind or heart, we pretend nothing happened, as if putting a cast on an inner break somehow makes us weak—especially true for someone who teaches this stuff to others. We know how to deal with grief, right? We don't need help from someone else to deal with our emotions. We got this. Knowing the truth doesn't necessarily prevent grief from getting the better part of someone who deals with it every day.

When most people hear the "D" word, meaning depression, they automatically think of a severely depressed person in a white straitjacket requiring institutionalization. In the Victorian era of medicine, doctors extensively used the straitjacket as a form of treatment for mental illness. They physically restrained depressed individuals so they didn't harm themselves and/or others.

In reality, depression may be described as feeling sad, or down in the dumps. Whether we admit it or not, most of us feel depressed to some degree at one point or another in our lives. Usually, the emotions are short lived, and then we pull ourselves up and move forward. Sadness is a normal response to life's transitions, setbacks, or disappointments. So we expect to feel some degree of sadness after experiencing a traumatic event in life.

Dr. Elisabeth Kubler-Ross was a psychiatrist who pioneered the concept of providing grief counseling to the dying. In her groundbreaking book, *On Death and Dying*, she coined the five stages of grief. She believed those nearing death routinely experienced denial, anger, bargaining,

DEPRESSION, and acceptance.

According to Kubler-Ross, depression is the stage where grief enters our lives on a deeper level. An overwhelming emotion, this part of grief feels like it will last forever. Kubler-Ross taught an important lesson—depression in its mildest form, is a natural part of the grieving process. It is important to understand that feeling depressed does not signal mental illness. It's the appropriate response to a great loss in your life, such as the death of a loved one, an illness, a divorce, the loss of a job, home, or car. All of these situations can cause sadness for anyone.

Have you ever stuffed your feelings of sadness? If yes, give yourself permission to feel the emotion and cleanse your body of grief. When you take the time to feel your sadness, you let the sadness work itself out of your system. All emotions must be felt and allowed to pass through our bodies. Not allowing yourself to feel sadness deters your healing process. Jesus Himself experienced sadness after Herod murdered John the Baptist. We find the story in Matthew 14:12-13. John's disciples took his body, buried it, and went to tell Jesus about it. When He heard the news, He withdrew by boat privately to a solitary place.

At times in our life, we need to withdraw privately and

allow ourselves to feel the emotions that lay dormant in our bodies. If Jesus took the time to withdraw when He suffered a loss, how much more do we need to do the same? He set an example for us to follow. Know that it is your responsibility to protect your own mental health.

Educate yourself on mental health topics. Undealt with emotions can lead to clinical depression, which is a mood disorder where feelings of sadness, anger, loss, anxiety, or frustration interfere with everyday life for months—or maybe even a lifetime. Sadness doesn't debilitate you, clinical depression does. Considered a mental illness, this type of depression doesn't mean you are mentally ill. One can remain functional to some degree and be clinically depressed. So, if the dark cloud of depression hovers over you for an extended period of time and you feel emotionally stuck, perhaps it's time to be aggressive in your treatment and seek professional help to determine your plan of care.

Dealing with emotional pain can be harder than coping with physical pain. Sometimes it's hard to wrap your mind around what's happening in your life in spite of all your knowledge.

This became my reality for the very first time in my life.

I didn't have the means to cope with my emotional pain. After my husband announced his desire to move on in life without me, I immediately started making mental notes of what I needed to do to care for "Tonya."

Even though my educational background is in social work and counseling, the spirit of depression immediately came and took up residence in my home. That Friday night, February 24, 2012, at 8:20pm, I began to write a "to do" list while sitting on the couch listening to him tell me "I no longer have the capacity to be married to you any longer."

I thought to myself, "What does THAT mean?" I kept awaiting a detailed explanation of what he meant, but it never came. I battled with that statement until a year later when I began to connect the dots of my broken and dysfunctional marriage. All I know is that statement left me feeling worthless and less than a human being with feelings and emotions worth recognition. Although his words devastated me, I must admit relief washed over me at the same time. He FINALLY verbalized what I felt exude from him for quite some time. In an effort to salvage our marriage I often used the analogy of the Grand Canyon— enormous, deep and wide. On many occasions, I told him, "The grand canyon between us is getting bigger." Meaning, we needed to honestly communicate with one another and address some issues in our marriage or we would fall into the canyon, never to come out.

He disconnected from me as if I was his enemy. I constantly compared myself to the female character in the movie *Sleeping with the Enemy*. Many times, I wanted to run from the marriage. I'm quite sure he wanted to run away too. But I made a covenant to God and to him. Besides, he was my prince charming I waited for all of my life. I simply could not walk away without trying to mend the pieces of my broken dream. Yet, both parties of a covenant must fight to keep it. Without both partners on board, the resolve dissipates. And the next steps flow as easily as making a list. Well, my "to do" list contained only three instructions.

• Inform my immediate family, friends, and spiritual leaders of what's about to go down in our lives.

• Call my primary care physician first thing Monday morning to schedule an appointment to get "happy pills." In my opinion, my husband just sucked the life out of me and took my "happy." How can a social worker tell others to "be happy" when she has none of her own happiness left?

• Contact an attorney to represent me in the divorce, because I didn't have energy to represent myself.

I had the right answers, knew the right steps to take. And I put them in action. But as news of my marriage ending circulated, I didn't expect the impact. Debilitated to the point where I couldn't do anything but go to work, I walked around in a daze, doing just enough to make it through the weekend.

Monday morning I made it to work, my proverbial marbles out of whack. Uncertain whether some slipped out of my head completely in the last few days, I knocked timidly on my supervisor's door.

"Got a minute?"

"Hey Tonya. How was..." She stopped, stood up and moved toward me. "What's going on?"

"I need to let you know what's going on, in case you notice a difference in my work performance. I fully expect not to perform at my optimum level."

My palms sweated. I tried to swallow down my emotions, but the harder I tried, the faster my heart throbbed. The fog in my brain vibrated, making clear thought almost impossible.

Holding back the ache inside, I took a deep breath and

rushed past the words. "My husband no longer has the capacity to be married to me any longer." I sank into a chair. "I don't even know what that means." I propped my head up with my hand, uncertain I could hold it up without help.

My supervisor rushed to my side. "Oh Tonya, I'm so sorry. Don't worry about work. You just take care of yourself right now."

And I did take care of myself—at least I did all of the things I knew to do. I started going to counseling and taking antidepressants. As a minister of the Gospel of Christ, many fellow believers expressed their displeasure of my actions. They stated that my self-care showed a lack of faith in God. I kindly disagreed then, and I still do. Sometimes, we need wise counsel to overcome traumatic events. We don't question getting a prescription to heal physically from pain. Few people reject temporary use of painkillers when a broken bone first starts the healing process. My heart broke as deeply as any bone. Before long, I left the church, filled with the shame of a broken marriage and accused of weak faith.

The Bible speaks on both counseling and medicinal methods. Let's look at what the scripture shares about it.

Interestingly, the writer of Proverbs believed in seeking out the advice of a wise man. "For by wise counsel you will wage your own war, and in a multitude of counselors there is safety." (Proverbs 24:6, NKJV)

"Where there is no counsel, the people fall; but in the multitude of counselors there is safety." (Proverbs 11:14, NKJV)

The prophet Ezekiel encouraged the use of medicines. "Along the bank of the river, on this side and that, will grow all kinds of trees used for food; their leaves will not wither, and their fruit will not fail. They will bear fruit every month, because their water flows from the sanctuary. Their fruit will be for food, and their leaves for medicine." (Ezekiel 47:12, NKJV)

Divorce and depression are two topics considered taboo in the church. In African American cultures, the social norm says ignore these subjects as well. If we don't talk about it, depression will go away. Wrong answer! It's time for theology and psychology to collaborate in providing healing to the total man. So free yourself from religion and go get the help you need.

Various physical conditions can contribute to depression. In some cases bipolar, postpartum depression, biochemical imbalance, certain medications, drugs, improper food and genetic vulnerability affect the brain. Based on research and statistical data, individuals with a history of depressed family members are two times more vulnerable to depression.

So, that Monday morning before work, I called to schedule an appointment with my primary care physician. Number two on the take care of me to do list. She had no openings until 3 weeks later. With the weight of depression hanging over me, there was a great possibility I wouldn't be alive to make that appointment.

Desperate times calls for desperate measures. So I took the first available appointment with another doctor in her office.

I arrived at the doctor's office as scheduled. The doctor began to ask a series of questions, which began with "Are you suicidal?"

I know what it feels like when clients are dishonest, so in an attempt to remain truthful, I replied, "Yes, I am suicidal."

She continued. "What method would you use?"

I thought for a moment. "I would use pills because I don't like pain. A gunshot or stab wound would NOT be my choice of demise."

A blank stare appeared on her face, creeping across in a slow arc and stealing her words in the process.

I finally realized I had just asked her for antidepressants! I laughed. "It's the emotional pain that's talking. I'm not going to kill myself; I just want those happy pills."

She didn't see any humor in the situation. The doctor would not give me the antidepressants until I signed a suicide contract agreeing to go to a mental health behavioral hospital if the thought of killing myself arose again.

"I want to admit you to Millwood Mental Health Hospital—today.

"We don't need to do that. I'm just going through a tough time and need a little help. The pills will make me better." Like most people, I thought to myself, "That place is for crazy people, and I'm not crazy!"

I signed the contract, got my prescription for some happy pills and quickly exited her exam room.

As time went on, I continued to decline and exhibit signs of clinical depression. I experienced a considerable amount of weight loss, uncontrollable crying, reduced level of interest in the outside world, increase in anxiety, feelings of fatigue, and the inability to concentrate—and yes, I was still suicidal.

Thirty days passed and I hadn't eaten a morsel of food. Family and friends encouraged me to eat. I had no appetite for physical food; I just wanted the pain to end. I heard rumors I was sick with AIDS because I dropped so much weight so fast. That one left me confused. Why would I have AIDS of all things?

The tension of depression began to mound upon my mind as if an elephant was sitting on my head. During our separation, countless individuals contacted me and shared vital information my husband shared with them in times past. He was not happy in the marriage and had not been for a long time. My life felt like a jigsaw puzzle with the pieces slowly coming together. I began to realize I wasn't crazy for feeling disconnected in this marriage.

I must mention three encounters that sent me in a downward spiral into the black hole of suicidal thoughts. The first two encounters came when two gay guys (on separate occasions) called me and stated they heard my husband and I were separated and headed to divorce court. Their initial question knocked me to my knees.

Each one of them asked, "Have you had an AIDS test?"

"What? Where is this AIDS thing coming from?"

Both of them shared, "The gay community is a close-knit community."

One of them stated my husband's name had been traveling within that arena. Marbles rolled around, bumping together before a few more slipped out.

Numb from the words that came out of their mouths I followed their instructions without hesitation and scheduled an appointment with my physician to have a battery of tests done—for my sanity.

Pins and needles poked me, some a mere annoyance and others stabbing deep while I awaited the results. The reports came back—all tests were negative. However, I grappled with this in my head over and over again, trying to make sense of something my brain wouldn't comprehend.

The third encounter that heavily impacted me was when I received a report from the street committee. The report stated that after I left the church, my husband expressed over the pulpit, "The church will roll on."

My mind snapped!

I quickly understood the TV show, *Snapped*. The tears gushed like a never-ending flood. I curled up in the fetal position in the corner of what I turned into a prayer room, rocking back and forth in despair. Questions surged, flooding my mind, drowning me.

"How can the church that I helped build, roll on as if I didn't exist?"

"As the pastor's wife, did I ever matter to him and the people?"

"Do they not see that I'm dying over here by myself? Where are those people that said they loved me?"

"Was I nothing more than a trophy wife? Was my marriage real? Is God really real?"

I cried out in desperation. "God don't you see me hurting?" The pain rushed in, overwhelming me. I couldn't move, pleading for God to make it stop—make it all stop.

At that moment, I heard the physician's voice. "If you think of taking your own life, do not call me. Go straight to Millwood Mental Health Hospital."

I got up off the floor, called my sister, and said, "Take me to the hospital—now."

## Scripture: Isaiah 50:10 NKJV

*"Let him who walks in darkness and has not light trust in the name of the Lord and rely on his God."*

## Grief nugget:

*"Confront any loss and emotional pain in your life, allowing yourself to mourn and to be healed."*

~Tonya Cunningham, LBSW, MA

based on Ecclesiastes 3:4

## Self-Reflection:

How do you define depression?

Do you give yourself permission to be sad?

Have you ever known someone who was seriously depressed?

Would you consider taking antidepressants? Why or Why not?

# CHAPTER 6
# THE MESSAGE AT MILLWOOD

*"Man, when you lose your laugh you lose your footing."*

*"He knows that you have to laugh at the things that hurt you just to keep yourself in balance, just to keep the world from running you plumb crazy."*

*"I been silent so long now it's gonna roar out of me like floodwaters and you think the guy telling this is ranting and raving my God; you think this is too horrible to have really happened, this is too awful to be the truth! But, please. It's still hard for me to have a clear mind thinking on it. But it's the truth even if it didn't happen."*

~Ken Kesey, *One Flew Over the Cuckoo's Nest*

These are a few of my favorite quotes from the 1975 movie[3] based on the 1962 novel *One Flew Over the Cuckoo's Nest* by Ken Kesey. [4]

---

[3] (Michael Douglas, 1975)

[4] (Kesey, 1962)

In the movie, a character by the name of Chief Bromden, serves as the narrator. He's been a patient in a mental hospital in Oregon for 10 years. He shares his view of what happens on a day-to-day basis in the hospital. On any given day, the happenings on the ward vary. Commonalities range from total chaos, screaming, aimless walking, drooling from the mouth, rocking back and forth in a rocking chair and a host of other behaviors creating an environment defining the term crazy.

Nurse Ratched monitors the all-male mental patients. A former military nurse, she runs the ward with an iron fist. Nurse Ratched doesn't use the most effective form of therapy to rehab the patients. All about order, she divides the men into two categories during daily group meetings. Acutes—those who can be cured. And chronics—those destined to remain confined and without hope of a cure.

She encourages the acutes to attack the chronics in hopes of getting them to buckle and submit to her dictatorship.

Then one day, Randle McMurphy, is admitted to the ward and changes the atmosphere into an even more chaotic arena. He challenges Nurse Ratched's authority by enticing the other patients to defy her rules. They all rebel against her forceful treatment. Nurse Ratched loses control and yells at them. From the perspective of Chief Bromden, an outsider looking in on this scene, everybody in the mental hospital was crazy—including the staff.

This movie depicts the perception some people have of mental hospitals. I admit that until recently, in their negative view of mental health care, mainstream society skewed my view of these kinds of facilities too.

After coming to a place of losing my laughter, I didn't care about my perception nor the opinion of others. I just wanted the emotional pain to stop. Honestly, I didn't want to die, but when my world came crushing down on me, I didn't know HOW to LIVE. As the sadness overwhelmed me, every ounce of physical strength oozed out of my body. Lifting an arm to comb my hair required more energy than I had. How could I fight with my mind, spirit or emotions if I couldn't even lift my arm?

Giving up on life sounded easier. In my depressed mind, suicide was the lesser of two evils. You don't have to make too many decisions, other than the mode of your demise. But how do you make a decision like that when your mind won't respond? When frankly, you don't have enough impetus left to think about it long enough to decide. And even if you decided, carrying out your plan means moving more than an inch.

After calling my sister to take me to the hospital, my immediate villagers rallied around and transported me, while others met me there.

On Sunday, April 1, 2012 at approximately 8:00pm, I admitted myself to Millwood Hospital Center for Mental Health and Chemical Dependency Care. Their tagline says, "We believe in People."

Little did I know that a paradigm shift was about to take place in my life, empowering me to be the strong, confident woman of God I am today. Then again, in that state, I didn't know much of anything.

Walking in the doors, I expected a crazy atmosphere. I didn't care. That was the crazy part. I didn't care—about anything. My emotions no longer registered. Like a car with an empty gas tank, I barely moved—so low emotionally I literally felt like I was about to fly over the Cuckoo's Nest. But I didn't see any of the craziness I anticipated.

On arrival, the intake personnel led me to a room. The admission process. I knew this.

I dragged myself into the room with legs like a jellyfish. The emotional hurricane raging in my body, mind and soul drained the last bit of stamina from me. I immediately sat in the chair and laid my head on the round table before me, waiting for the barrage of questions and discussion about patient rights, consent, plan of care, discharge plan, etc.

I signed every document without reading a single one. As a social worker, I knew the drill. I couldn't be crazy. How could I understand everything going on if I didn't have full control of my mind?

I was anxious to get back behind those locked doors and get the help I so desperately wanted. I needed a clinical authority to tell me I wasn't crazy for feeling the way I felt. Like Dorothy in the movie, *The Wiz*, I was ready to ease on down the road where the Wizard had all of the answers.

My sisters and friend accompanied me to the room while other family members stayed in the waiting area. Dismay, hurt, fear and anger enveloped their faces. The strong one didn't look strong. Each of their faces held a question— was I going to be all right?

Life stripped me of everything—love, marriage, my family, my church, my friends, laughter, joy, peace, my identity—and now apparently my mind. There I was again; being stripped of things I couldn't take with me. In the locked unit, I had nothing. No cellphone, purse, or jewelry.

So my family took those items for me. The hospital let me keep the clothes on my back, a few clothing items I brought from home and a jacket my friend gave me because the building felt like the North Pole.

At that point, I willingly gave up whatever I needed to release. I had to get to a peaceful place.

The time came for me to say goodbye to my family. With each hug, their sheer helplessness melted into me. With all of their love and support, they couldn't fix me. I alone had to surrender to God's will and walk the green mile for myself, by myself.

Without hesitation, I turned towards the huge double doors of the locked unit and walked into a dark abyss.

We entered the unit around 10:00pm. Behind closed doors, patients slept. No screaming or yelling. No aimless walking or rocking. The empty halls echoed the hollowness of my heart.

If you know anything about locked units, patients do nothing without permission. The staff escorted me to the desk where a nurse administered my nighttime regimen for depression and anxiety. I swallowed the pills and awaited instructions.

Finally, I was in a place where I didn't have to make a

decision. I didn't mind that at all.

The nice lady led me to my room. "Get some rest, Tonya. You'll receive a schedule in the morning." Ahhhh. The regimen in the locked unit. "We serve meals at scheduled times and join others for group time. Of course we have some times to relax and play games if you want," she said. "You'll see a doctor tomorrow as well. But for now, just sleep."

Every minute of the day, scheduled. No decisions. No time alone. No worry about hurting myself or anyone else. I nodded and inched into bed.

For the first time since February, I slept the entire night.

The next morning, I awakened to the voice of a cheerful staff member. "It's time to get up, shower and head to the group room."

"Okay," I mumbled, not wanting to wake up yet.

My roommate introduced herself and gave me a crash course of the dos and don'ts of the unit. She told me who to stay away from and who was safe to connect with. An immediate connection formed from our common place of hurt. We both needed resolve to move forward in life. My roommate, a total stranger, became my guardian angel and protected me during my stay.

We headed to the group area and waited for an escort to the cafeteria and breakfast. After we ate, we had group time, during which I met the rest of the patients on the unit. The goal of admission to a mental behavioral hospital is to utilize medication and therapy to stabilize the patient so he or she can cope with life in a healthy manner. Every day in the group session, we worked on a safety crisis plan that included triggers, stressors, warning signs, etc. We also developed a plan for healthy coping skills and goal setting.

I spent 6 nights and 6 days (Sunday night to Saturday afternoon) at Millwood. From a biblical standpoint, six is the number of man. Meaning, I entered the hospital as the flesh girl Tonya but was about to be discharged as the born again Woman of God Tonya. I had no idea I was about to have a spiritual encounter with God IN the mental hospital. Do such things really happen?

I felt like Joseph in the Bible, a man with a divine purpose whose name means "increase." Even during his journey from the pit to the palace, the Bible frequently mentions, "the Lord was with Joseph." God's hand rested on Joseph's life because he kept his focus on God, and everyone around him saw clear evidence of the Creator's favor on this man. Joseph didn't understand why the Lord chose that path for him, and he didn't necessarily like it. But he never wavered in his faith, and God used him greatly.

During my tenure, I didn't realize I had an uncommon advantage in the mental hospital. The Spirit of the living God was ever present with me. His "favor" dripped off me like raindrops falling from the roof. The staff gave me extra snacks, extra food and extra time to complete assignments. Eventually they allowed me extra time for sleep.

As I walked through the halls of the locked unit, I sensed a light shining over my head. I looked over at the other patients and didn't see this light. What in the world was going on? A deep darkness hung in the air all around me, yet this blazing bright light continuously lingered over my head.

The surreal light seemed real to me, but in a hospital designed for mental illness...

The other patients, my Millwood friends, noticed the favor, and they asked about it. "How come you get all this special treatment? Why do you get all the extra sleep?"

"What are you talking about?"

"You slept for an entire day, and they didn't make you wake up."

"Really?"

"You fell asleep Tuesday afternoon and didn't wake up until Wednesday afternoon. Literally all day, girl."

Clueless about the vast amount of time I slept, or why the staff allowed it, I knew something amazing happened during the 24-hour period.

During the day of sleep, I encountered God.

I remember laying in the bed, swaddled in a blanket because I was cold. Sometime in the night, a warm sensation fell all over my body, from the top of my head to the bottom of my feet. That blazing light burst over me only, not the remainder of the room. I literally felt God holding me in His arms, letting me know I would be all right. Actually better than before because He touched me.

In a matter of 24 hours, God peeled off the layers of hurt and fear, and He downloaded His plan for my life. He reconnected me to Him.

In the middle of the encounter, sadness washed over me. As a pastor's wife, I didn't even realize I unplugged from God. So busy doing the work of "church," I somehow disconnected from the Source, God! Like so many today, I did church instead of becoming the church. I repented in that place of closeness with the Father.

I felt so deeply in my spirit that God now owned complete control of my life. For real! Every fiber of my being quivered, begging for release. Begging to jump up and down with joy. I wanted to tell my roommate, but I couldn't move. So I surrendered all to the Lord and rested the remainder of the time. During this spiritual experience, I received the 'Message at Millwood.' God told me He was there with me at the lowest point of my life, and that nothing was a mistake. It was all in His plan (Jeremiah 29:11.)

When I woke up the next day, I felt like Sleeping Beauty, all refreshed. I didn't know how long I slept. It seemed only a few minutes passed, but at that point, my Millwood friends informed me I slumbered for an entire day.

I woke up with a new determination to get better. I summoned my social worker.

"It's time for me to be discharged," I said bluntly.

I immediately stopped taking the medication. I don't recommend this for others. Sudden stops of some drugs can cause serious damage. God took me on this journey and dealt with me in a specific way. Every journey looks different, coming from a creative God.

Of course, the social worker, along with the psychiatrist

and other staff, discouraged my discharge at that point. I remained adamant that they release me ASAP.

I felt resurrection coming in my life!

I was not going to leave against medical advice, because I wanted the documents to show they discharged me. I wanted God to get the full glory for this miraculous healing of my mind.

They called a family meeting with my two sisters and informed them of my desire to go home by Saturday. With all the mess in my mind, I failed to remember a crucial fact.

Easter fell on that Sunday!

That's why I felt the urgency in my spirit to get out by Saturday. I determined to be in God's house on that Easter Sunday because of what He did for me, raising me up to tell of His goodness.

Exhilaration bombarded the weariness in my muscles and bones. An inexplicable desire to run like a child flashed through me. After the care plan meetings with family and psychiatrist, they decided to discharge me under suicide watch. I could go home, but someone had to stay with me 24/7 until the psychiatrist lifted the watch. They also instructed my sisters to remove knives, scissors and all sharp objects from my home.

I signed the contract even if I didn't agree. I knew one thing for sure. God wanted me out of the hospital on Saturday and attending church on Sunday. I was willing to do whatever I needed to do to get out of the hospital, to go where I said I would never go again—church.

When I traversed the threshold of the locked unit on Sunday night, I had no idea the walk down THAT aisle in the form of a hallway was the best walk I'd ever experience. I was about to walk into my season of increase (Joseph) and resurrection (Jesus.)

Don't get me wrong. Nothing around me looked like an increase in my life. But I kept on walking and doing my work to get better, submitting to those who cared for me because I couldn't care for myself.

## Scripture: Gen 39:21 NKJV

*"But the Lord was with Joseph and showed him mercy, and He gave him favor in the sight of the keeper of the prison."*

## Grief nugget:

*"Once you accept the existence of God…then you are caught forever with His presence at the center of all things. You are also caught with the fact that man is a creature who walks in two worlds and traces upon the wall of his cave the wonders and the nightmare experiences of his spiritual pilgrimage."*

~Morris West, *The Clowns of God*

## Self-Reflection:

What do you do to nurture your mental health?

Have you ever received any type of counseling?

# CHAPTER 7
# IT'S TIME TO EXCEL

The FMLA (Family and Medical Leave Act) entitles eligible employees of covered employers to take unpaid, job-protected leave for specified family and medical reasons with continuation of group health insurance coverage under the same terms and conditions as if the employee had not taken leave. Eligible employees are entitled to:

• Twelve workweeks of leave in a 12-month period for:

• The birth of a child and to care for the newborn child within one year of birth;

• The placement with the employee of a child for adoption or foster care and to care for the newly placed child within one year of placement;

• To care for the employee's spouse, child, or parent who

has a serious health condition;

• A serious health condition that makes the employee unable to perform the essential functions of his or her job;

• Any qualifying exigency arising out of the fact that the employee's spouse, son, daughter, or parent is a covered military member on "covered active duty;" or

• Twenty-six workweeks of leave during a single 12-month period to care for a covered service member with a serious injury or illness if the eligible employee is the service member's spouse, son, daughter, parent, or next of kin (military caregiver leave). [5]

For your reading pleasure, I thought it necessary to include FMLA facts in this chapter. Most of us working individuals are aware of the Act but never utilize the benefit because we believe we can't afford to take off work without pay.

As a result of experiencing the life-changing event of a divorce, for the very first time in my life, I applied for FMLA. In order to continue progression in recovery, Millwood Hospital referred me to a center next door to the hospital for Intensive Outpatient Therapy. My doctor admitted to the Excel Center on April 11, 2012, and I

[5] (United States Department of Labor, 2015)

completed the program on May 9, 2012.

Diagnosis: single episode major depression.

The first day at Excel started with a turbulent admission process that hit me like a category five tornado, popping up out of a clear blue sky.

During my intake interview, the initial questions twirled around me and slammed debris against my brain. Innocent questions—deadly emotional turmoil.

"What's your marital status and do you have pastoral support?"

Now, I'm angry. My husband was my pastor too! I lost not only my life companion but my spiritual covering as well.

I swallowed the anger bubbling up in me and quickly answered those two questions. "Divorced and no. Can we proceed with the interview?"

Later, the admissions counselor asked if I wanted to attend the faith-based group or clinical group.

Spontaneously, I responded, "Clinical." I wanted nothing to do with church ever again. Then I paused and asked, "Is the faith-based group super religious, churchy?"

I moved forward in my seat, ready for him to say yes. Ready to run as far away from that as I could. Although I had an awesome spiritual encounter with God in Millwood, I was still angry with Him, my soon to be ex-husband and anybody remotely associated with him.

The admissions counselor assured me the faith-based group was not over the top religious. "The counselor simply provides patients with scripture in addition to theoretic perspectives." He paused, eyeing me. "Patients are afforded one opportunity to move once from one group to another within their treatment plan."

Drumroll please. With extreme hesitation, I elected to attend the faith-based group, which was already in session. I could always change my mind.

He escorted me down the hallway to the group therapy room. Once again, I felt like I walked the Green Mile, fearing what and who waited on the other side of that door.

I prayed silently. "Lord, PLEASE don't let me know anybody in this room!" I just wanted a safe place with total strangers to continue my healing.

As we passed the vending machines, I noticed a huge wicker basket full of marbles sitting on the countertop. The counselor walked too fast for me to inquire about the basket. So I thought to myself, "What in the world are those marbles for?"

He directed me to an available seat in the back of the room. One of the patients talked about her experience at Excel. As I listened further, I realized this was what they called the "Marbling-Out Ceremony."

In our society, the phrase "losing their marbles" means going crazy. After matriculating through the program, the counselors ask that you choose two marbles from the wicker basket on the countertop. One should represent how you were on admission to Excel, and the other marble should represent how you felt after completing the program.

The Marbling-Out ceremony, an emotional yet beautiful depiction of her transformation from brokenness to wholeness, touched the group. Almost everyone in the room dabbed at their eyes, including me.

Break-time arrived, bringing the presumption of a much-needed moment of relief. A jovial woman came up to me. In any other time and place, I might have found her excitement contagious.

"I know you! You are the First Lady at my cousin's church!"

She was so happy to meet me. I didn't have the heart, neither the energy, to tell her I was no longer the First

Lady.

I recognized her as the one who marbled out. I couldn't burst her bubble with horrible news.

It took ALL the strength within me not to explode in tears as she stood before me, bouncing with delight. I plastered a smile across my face, nodding and uttering "um-hmm" when appropriate. After what seemed like an hour, someone approached her with congratulatory words, relinquishing her hold on me.

I bolted from the room and ran to my car. Safe inside, I screamed uncontrollably at God! "Can I PLEASE have someplace where nobody knows that I am….well, that I was a Pastor's wife?"

Heartbroken from her greeting, I determined NOT to return for the afternoon session. Somehow, I mustered up enough courage to go back in the room.

A different counselor facilitated the group and gave opportunity for newcomers, like me, to introduce ourselves to the group. I barely uttered my name before the tears started flowing again, to the point where everyone in the group surrounded and hugged me. Then, they prayed for me. They gave me permission to be hurt and angry about the demise of my marriage.

Realization dropped over me. I sat in a room full of pastors, chaplains, evangelists, prophets, and teachers that day. People from the church—and all of us, patients in Outpatient Therapy!

I wasn't the only one who had been to hell and back. I met and developed life-long relationships with some beautiful people in that group. To this day, I am friends with several of them.

Just as in Millwood, I had an encounter with God at Excel. Many of my counterparts in the group approached me and said, "What are you doing here? You don't belong in a place like this. Pick yourself up, dust yourself off and get out of here!"

An older gentleman, a chaplain, approached me after my first day in group. He said, "Pastor Tonya, I don't know who you are, but God told me to tell you, He's gonna make you spill the beans. Now I don't know what that means, but I believe that you know what I'm referring to. Rest assured that God sees and knows what's going on."

The anointing on this man's life emanated from him. I attempted to avoid him to keep from getting a prophetic word. I wasn't ready to hear any prophecy. Like a magnet drawing him to me, every day he sought me out and shared the word of the Lord with me.

As God was with me in Millwood, He was with me in Excel as well. This angel of God in outpatient therapy strengthened me daily.

After my initial encounter with the elderly gentleman, God spoke to me and said, "Consecrate yourself. Don't put another piece of meat in your mouth until this divorce is final because no flesh will be glorified during this healing journey."

He also instructed me to contact 12 prayer warriors to come to my house and pray for me and to pray over the house. These warriors consisted of pastors, evangelists and prophets from DFW to Oklahoma.

In my weakened state of mind, I barely kept my head above water. I certainly couldn't pray. So I surrounded myself with people who could until God empowered me to pray for myself again.

I heeded to the instructions of God and began to call and text the 12 people He downloaded in my spirit. They all responded in the affirmative and adjusted their schedules to meet my need. Biblically speaking, the number 12 indicates governmental order. My life was about to be put into the order according to God's purpose and plan for me. Each of them came loaded and ready with an Ephesians 6:12 perspective. "For we do not wrestle against flesh and blood, but against principalities, against powers, against the rulers of the darkness of this age, against spiritual hosts of wickedness in the heavenly places."

For two solid weeks, different people consistently prayed in my home. So much peace surrounded my home and me. I felt like Obed-Edom in the bible. He housed the Ark of the Covenant in his house for three months before moving it on to Jerusalem. The bible makes reference that God blessed Obed-Edom and his entire household during the time the Ark of the Covenant resided with him.

I was so blessed because of the prayers that went up in my home as a sweet smelling savor unto our God. After prayer with my spiritual mother, she instructed me to keep a journal near my bedside. She told me God was going to be speaking to me mightily. She was so right! During this time, the spiritual encounters with God continued in my home through dreams and visions. And as sure as she is a woman of God, the dreams and visions came gushing in like a tidal wave.

I was up and down all night long the first three or four nights of being home on suicide watch. On April 12, 2012 at 2:30am, I experienced the first of many spiritual encounters. In this dream, I balled up in the fetal position, stuck in the birth canal. I so desperately needed help being birthed.

As the Spirit of the Lord awakened me, I found myself literally curled in the fetal position in the middle of my bed. His gentle voiced ministered to me, "You don't need overnight supervision any longer."

I journaled what the Spirit of God said and woke up my middle sister to show her. "See, God says to call off the suicide watch. I have to be left alone so God can finish His work in me."

I went on and shared with her that the fetal position represented a tight place in my life, and only God could birth me out of that place and into a brand new world.

She agreed, so we called off the suicide watch without notifying my psychiatrist. What I dealt with at this point encompassed the spiritual. Later, my psychiatrist released me from his care.

Disclaimer: As with the sudden end to my medication, I don't recommend that others follow this regimen. Again, God dealt with me this way during my healing process, but He chooses appropriate paths for each person, including the intense care of a qualified professional, guiding his patient to healing.

Another encounter came when I experienced what I call a "death walk."

Early one morning, God awakened me. I walked around my home, body bowed over as if I carried a cross. No matter how hard I tried, I couldn't straighten my body. So I slowly walked, step-by-step, with feet as heavy as cement. As I walked, tears streamed from my eyes. I couldn't utter a word. I walked and wailed, walked and wailed, walked and wailed for a while, until He released me.

I feared sharing these encounters with everybody, concerned they would think I was crazy. I carefully selected with whom I shared these experiences. Nothing disappoints more than sharing exciting news with someone, and he or she doesn't respond with enthusiasm. I shared this experience with a pastor friend, and she ministered to me, reminding me of the death walk Jesus endured on His way to Calvary.

The encounters continued. Perhaps one day, God will release me to share more of them. For now, the ones chosen for this book provide a sprinkling of God's work in my life, as He healed my heart.

The Excel Center helped me process the trauma of divorce from a spiritual perspective as well as a theoretical perspective. Both are vital for total healing. The counselors empowered us with information and homework on critical topics. Survival tactics, negative thinking and self-talk, the language of love, positive focus, anger, goal setting, gratitude, healthy boundaries, trials, fear, divorce, forgiveness, and emotional abuse glimpse the extensive list.

In addition to all God accomplished in my healing, I treasure the center's help as well. They provided tools and knowledge that brought healing from the past and wisdom for the future.

The date finally arrived for me to marble out. I chose two blue marbles—one dark blue with white specks and a light blue one with a gold omega symbol on it. The darker marble represented how I felt on admission to Excel. I was in a dark place in my life with glimpses of light and hope. The light blue marble speaks of serenity and peace.

I found that marble after digging down to the bottom of the wicker basket. It was as if that blazing bright light shining on me in Millwood illuminated that marble!

The Spirit of God said, "I am your Omega! I am with you, even in this."

In that moment, I yelled out, "I got my marbles back!"

I decreed, "One day I will preach that message and write a book about it."

The excitement of getting our marbles back spread across the room like wildfire. Others joined my declaration with a resounding "I got my marbles back!"

After completion of that program, the doctors released my return to full-time work. During such time, I continued in counseling May 14, 2012 until June 27, 2012.

June 28, 2012 marked the ninth anniversary of my marriage—a marriage in the middle of dissolution. To my surprise, my counselor discharged me on that date.

"Are you sure I'm ready?" I asked. I felt a little anxious about the anniversary date.

She chuckled and said, "Tonya, you are more than ready. You can continue to come if you want me to take your money. The only time you may need to come back is when you start dating again so I can teach you how to date in a healthy manner."

My pilgrimage continued under the care of my psychiatrist who quickly discharged me as well and my primary care physician.

The divorce was final in November of 2012, and I

celebrated being a vegetarian because of the 7-month long consecration.

## Scripture: Psalm 103:20 NKJV

*"Bless the Lord, you His angels, who excel in strength, who do His word, heeding the voice of His word."*

## Proverbs 31:29 NKJV

*"Many daughters have done well, but you excel them all."*

## Grief nugget:

"We Heal by Sharing!"

~Terrie M. Williams, Black Pain

## Self-Reflection:

Have you shared your story with anyone?

# CHAPTER 8
# CHURCHLESS IN FORT WORTH

*Sleepless in Seattle* is a 1993 American romantic comedy-drama film about a Chicago architect, named Sam Baldwin who loses his wife to cancer. He moves to Seattle, Washington with his 8-year-old son, Jonah, to start fresh. As Christmas rolls around, the memories of her love for Christmas dishearten Sam. The passing of time, about 18 months, haven't released him from the sting of her death and when night falls, he can't sleep. Sam is trying to figure out his identity without his Maggie.[6]

I, like Sam, experienced many sleepless nights due to the death of my marriage. Losing a loved one through physical demise or the death of a marriage can be devastating, turning your whole world upside down and out of balance.

[6] (Jeff Arch, 1993)

Physical death causing trauma makes sense. We don't always see a marriage ending as a reason for grief. In reality, both types of death create deep anguish.

The person you were, prior to the death, drifted out to sea and will never return. Therefore, in order to heal, it's important to stop expecting your "old self" to surface or come back to shore.

Why is it important to do this? Everything in your life changed, especially you. Your belief system, routines such as sleeping and eating, emotional stability, relationships and even your perception about life took on a different meaning.

Your comfort zone no longer exists, washed away in the relentless pounding of crashing waves. You need the creation of a new identity.

You may say, "But I don't want a new identity. I was fine just the way I was!"

Accepting the reality of a new situation does not mean you cut off the past and deny the existence of that person, relationship or thing. It simply means you build on the past to create a "new you."

When an ending occurs, it demands new beginnings. Before the fresh start happens, a period of transition takes place. During this time, the bereaved should closely examine what he or she lost and gained as a consequence of the ending. What actually changed? What continues the same? What is new? What experiences, roles, expectations, values, opportunities, and fantasies do we give up? What new ones can we assume?

Since I'm no longer a wife, am I a mother anymore? My daughter died and our adopted son elected to go with my husband, so who AM I now?

I didn't know what I liked. Kinda like Imani in the movie, *Coming to America,* Imani is the beautiful young lady trained from childhood to serve Prince Akeem.

She asked Prince Akeem, "Am I not all you dreamed I would be?"

His response affirmed her in her beauty, but he worried about her lack of an identity separate from him. He wanted to marry a woman who could think for herself.

Akeem said, "If we are going to be married, I thought we should talk to each other and get to know each other. So, what do you like?"

She responded as many wives do. "Whatever you like."[7]

Although we physically divorced, emotionally, I was still

[7] (Eddie Murphy, 1988)

attached to the life I knew for the last 10 years of being in covenant with this man. My emotions stay connected to my old life as a First Lady. I struggled with identity crisis. Because of the primary loss of my marriage, I experienced several secondary losses: my church, identity, family and friends.

For the first time in my life, I had no church home, which is foreign to me. I'm a church girl. I grew up in church. My DNA demanded I belonged there. Before these changes in my life, I never experienced not having a pastor—that trusted spiritual leader who guided me through difficult times.

Suddenly, I found myself divorced and without a pastor. I was churchless in Fort Worth.

Many Sundays I aimlessly drove around the city, wondering where to go. Where did I fit? Whom could I trust with me in this vulnerable state?

While I know this next statement isn't correct English, I'm gonna say it anyway, "Ain't nothing like church hurt!"

Like Sam in the movie, I initially thought I would soothe the pain of grief by relocating to another state where no one knows my old identity. Then I thought about my family and career—deeply rooted in this city. I should remain here because I needed a support network to help me through this healing process. I refer to that network as "My Village" taken from the concept of it takes a village to raise a child. It takes a village to help you heal when circumstances wound you emotionally. I needed help in processing feelings of abandonment, rejection, guilt, shame and so many more—emotions I didn't even know clung to my heart at first.

I could go to any church and receive a well-placed verse thrown in my direction by people who meant to comfort me. But when going through trials, you sometimes need a shoulder to cry on before you need a scripture.

I confess that transitioning from a First Lady was a little difficult. My flesh missed the few perks the title afforded me: reserved parking and seating alongside special recognition. No matter what time I arrived at church, I always had a seat and parking space awaiting me.

How easily I took those things for granted. With the title gone, I'm like everyone else. I have to find my own seat and parking. I laugh at the thought of such a silly notion. I got off track and fell prey to the church hype and didn't realize it. Long before my divorce, I became a victim of identity theft.

The enemy slipped in and stole my identity as a lady first and replaced it with the church image of a First Lady.

I repented before God, and He restored me. He revealed and gave me great appreciation for a simple fact. Although I'm no longer in the First Ladies club, I can rest and know I was a lady first before marriage.

They say hindsight is 20/20. Looking back on my tenure as a pastor's wife, I don't miss it. Today you can't pay me to be a First Lady. That seat is too expensive and the pay rate too low. I'll stick with finding my own seat. Seat for one please! Or better yet, I'm good just standing in the back.

I'm ashamed to admit I didn't know Tonya. I lost her. Yet another loss I mourned. Pastors and First Ladies from the DFW area and beyond called and offered themselves and their spouses as a covering for me until God transitioned me to a new church home. The sensitivity of what happened left raw, gaping wounds. I needed a new church where I could touch the pastor and his wife. I needed both of them to help nurture and love me back to life during the next phase of healing.

After a year of not attending church on a consistent basis, God led me to my next place of worship, Trinity

Harvest Church in Hurst, Texas, where I serve under the leadership of Senior Pastor Ray Taylor and First Lady Toni Nickerson Taylor. The precious people of that church loved me even when I came late, sat on the back row, and left early.

They pushed me out of my comfort zone through modern technology, and gave me an opportunity to do what I declared I would never do again. I said, "I will never mount another pulpit and minister to people." They gave me my voice back and ironically, my fellow ministers at the church refer to me as, "The Voice."

I love my new church home. I am no longer churchless.

## Scripture: Matt 16:18-19 The Message Bible

*"And now I'm going to tell you who you are, really are. You are Peter, a rock. This is the rock on which I will put together my church, a church so expansive with energy that not even the gates of hell will be able to keep it out. And that's not all. You will have complete and free access to God's kingdom, keys to open any and every door: no more barriers between heaven and earth, earth and heaven. A yes on earth is yes in heaven. A no on earth is no in heaven."*

## Grief nugget:

"After a loss, tunnel through the rubbish and discover your new normal, your new identity."

~ Tonya Cunningham, LBSW, MA

## Self-Reflection:

Identify times in your life that you have lost your identity.

Are you comfortable with your identity today? If not, what will you do to resolve that?

# CHAPTER 9
# HOARDING PAIN: BURIED ALIVE

The reality series, *Hoarders*[8] features stories of people who obsessively hoard to the point of personal crisis, of facing eviction, divorce, loss of relationships, or the removal of minor children from their home.

*Hoarding disorder is a persistent difficulty discarding or parting with possessions because of a perceived need to save them. A person with hoarding disorder experiences distress at the thought of getting rid of the items. Excessive accumulation of items, regardless of actual value, occurs. Hoarding often creates such cramped living conditions that homes may be filled to capacity, with only narrow pathways winding through stacks of clutter. Some people also collect animals, keeping dozens or hundreds of pets in unsanitary conditions because they can't care for them properly. Hoarding*

8 (Dave Severson, 2009-2012)

*ranges from mild to severe. In some cases, hoarding may not have much impact on your life, while in other cases it seriously affects your functioning on a daily basis. People with hoarding disorder often don't see it as a problem, making treatment challenging. But intensive treatment can help people with hoarding disorder understand their compulsions and live safer, more enjoyable lives.*

*~Mayo Clinic Staff*[9]

Several years ago a former coworker, who served as a hospice chaplain, asked that I come to the church she pastored and facilitate a grief group during the daytime hours. She planned to observe my group and then facilitate the group scheduled during evening hours.

As requested, I went and facilitated the well-attended grief group. During my teaching, I noticed my coworker, the pastor of a United Methodist Church, cried more than her parishioners did. She listened attentively to the information I shared on grief. As I began to wrap up, she dabbed away tears and let out a long sigh.

At the end of the group, she shared. "My husband died over 20 years ago. I have been hoarding grief!"

[9] (Mayo Clinic Staff, 2014)

As a female pastor in the United Methodist Denomination, no one gave her permission to mourn the death of her husband. She had to continue pastoring and caring for others in THEIR time of need, leaving her exposed to the cold elements of grief without release.

In February 2013, a year after my husband left, I watched the TV show *Hoarders* one evening. As I viewed the world of different people surrounded by possessions, the scales fell from my eyes.

I was a hoarder.

I didn't hold possessions like those I watched. I hoarded pain. Divorce came along and knocked down my twin towers, leaving me at ground zero. My life fell to involuntary reconstruction. I struggled in moving forward with my new life or new normal. I liked my old life as a pastor's wife, even with all of the dysfunction and stress. I clung to the old much like hoarders, who in spite of the massive amounts of chaos didn't necessarily want change.

Why did I like that life? It was in my comfort zone. I knew how to 'do church' because my parents raised me in the church. Life at home didn't bleed over to church—we kept it tucked away while we met the needs of everyone else.

Since the divorce, many people have asked if there were any warning signs. Of course there were. Initially I didn't see all the signs, and I didn't know exactly how to define the problem. Nevertheless, I knew something was off. My husband emotionally and intimately detached from me during most of the marriage. I asked him about the disconnection in hopes of receiving the truth. He never shared his heart with me.

As the years passed, the indifference intensified. How did we go from being happily married to divorce? Were we ever happily married? I hoarded these questions and many more in my mind, cluttering up my subconscious, and sometime conscious, thoughts.

Just after midnight one day, God awakened me. He downloaded strategies and knowledge. He ministered to my heart, revealing that I needed to release the pain. He walked me through layers, piles of mess. He showed me festering wounds, their stench covered in vain by pretty objects. And one by one, He pulled out the junk, threw it out and cleansed the spot where it lay. In the process, He showed me the vision of helping others do the same through "Release the Pain Sessions."

It's never easy when a marriage or significant

relationship ends. The break up brings agony, even when the relationship is no longer good. The disintegration represents a loss not just of the relationship but also of shared dreams and commitment. It's vital that we do our grief work because pain is a thief. Pain takes our energy and our joy. Grief requires both physical and emotional energy—hard work we sometimes don't want.

The term "grief work," coined by psychiatrist Erich Lindemann in 1944, describes the tasks and processes you must complete successfully in order to resolve your grief. The term shows grief doesn't resolve itself, but requires actively working to reconcile it in a healthy fashion.

In my opinion, the grief of death is easier to process than divorce. Death isn't a choice (unless you commit suicide.) When a spouse decides to leave the marriage, it's like viewing the body over and over again. I have found that to be true after four significant deaths in my life. My mentor, my baby, my mother, and my father all died.

NONE of them impacted me like the divorce did.

It became horrendously clear that I had to clean the emotional clutter from my closet. I identified the clutter.

• Abandonment – why did he leave?

• Rejection – what was wrong with me?

- Anger – why did he marry me?

- Forgiveness – can I forgive and forget?

In truth, I may never receive answers to these questions and many others; therefore, I must resolve within myself to clean the emotional clutter from my life.

Grief shared is grief diminished. Pain expressed is pain released.

I received a powerful message from the movie *Woman Thou Are Loosed*. Healing can't begin until the secrets come out. I had to be willing to expose myself, broken heart, broken mind, and broken soul because the horrible stench of decomposing flesh oozed out through the crevices of my life from hoarding pain.

The varmints of the questions listed above ate away at me like roaches in a hoarder's house. The thin onion layers of hurt could no longer be ignored. Hurt we don't deal with doesn't go away. It lies dormant, disguised as unprocessed pain until another traumatic event in life comes along and knocks the scab off the wound.

Healing is a journey and not a destination. So I continued doing my grief work by decluttering my life of any and everything that represented my old life. From furniture to wardrobe to friendships to life perspectives, unhealthy emotions and more. I detoxed my life and started a new one for real. God began the transformation of who He wanted me to be for Him, which is what we all should do, regardless of whether we are married or not.

When Jesus raised Lazarus from the dead, He set him free, but his grave clothes still bound him. I processed well on my grief journey by matriculating through Millwood and Excel, returning to full-time work, and conquering anxiety by adjusting to living alone. Even though these great things happened, abandonment, rejection, anger, unforgiveness, and fear still bound me.

I began to shed my grave clothes by tackling one emotion at a time and continued until I moved in complete freedom.

## Scripture: John 11:43-44 NKJV

*"Now when He had said these things, He cried with a loud voice, 'Lazarus, come forth! And he who had died came out bound hand and foot with grave clothes, and his face was wrapped with a cloth. Jesus said to them, 'Loose him, and let him go.'"*

## Grief nugget:

*"Be willing to sift through the ashes to find beauty in your pain. Beauty WILL rise again."*

~Tonya Cunningham, LBSW, MA

## Self-Reflection:

What emotions are you hoarding?

What do you plan to do to resolve those emotions and move forward in healing?

# CHAPTER 10
# BUTTERFLY

My grief education modules always included butterflies. After experiencing divorce, butterflies became an integral part of my life. My life and the life cycle of a butterfly ran parallel. A butterfly has four stages in its life cycle. The beautiful creature begins as an egg, hatches as a caterpillar, morphs to a chrysalis, and finally emerges as a butterfly. Each stage also has a different goal. The process by which the butterfly becomes an adult is called metamorphosis, which involves struggle, growth, and finally flight.

Just like butterflies, we strive toward our God-ordained path in our migration, flying forward in our purpose. Our lives also progress through struggle, growth and flying free.

When a butterfly is released to fly, that means it submitted to the process and endured all stages of its life cycle. Once the butterfly fights its way out of the cocoon, ready to fly, it's STILL not ready for release. Why? Because when it emerges, wet wings render the butterfly incapable of taking to the air.

When a butterfly first pokes through the shell of its chrysalis, the physical transformation from a caterpillar leaves it temporarily vulnerable to the waiting world. Not-quite-a-butterfly, it waits until the wings dry, and then it flies away. Experts warn never to touch the beautiful creature in this most fragile state. A single touch, even from the tip of the tiniest finger, permanently ruins the wings, and it will never learn to fly. The temptation to soar on the wind carries the danger of certain self-destruction unless the butterfly waits.

Likewise, we face the danger of trying to take off too soon, not quite ready, but thinking we can soar. Like the butterfly, we need time before taking flight.

Once the butterfly emerges, it takes four hours for the blood to infuse the wings. Then, it spreads its wings and flies. Four hours. In butterfly time, those hours chomp away a significant amount of their short lives. Yet they wait, quivering in the breeze, watching their friends flutter off, longing for their turn. Instinctively they know—delay is in their best interest. Rushing the process means certain death.

So, you have wings, but you are not ready to fly yet. It takes a while to figure out what God wants you to do, once you submit to Him. We usually require a lot longer than four hours for the blood to infuse our wings. Thank God for the blood of Jesus. According to Ephesians 1:7, "Although all have sinned, we have redemption through His blood, the forgiveness of sins." In the power of His blood, we can wait for perfect timing as He pumps the blood to the tips of our wings and prepares us for flight.

Biblically speaking, the number 4 represents balance. So while you wait, still getting ready to take off, your God-given vision grows balanced not only spiritually, but also emotionally, behaviorally, and financially.

"Then the Lord answered me and said, 'Write the vision and make it plain on tablets, that he may run who reads it.'" (Habakkuk 2:2 NKJV)

Once the blood fills the wings, it's time to fly! Nobody can release you like God can!

During the first century, we see a prime example of this concept. Recorded in Acts 16:25, Paul and Silas found themselves in a cocoon called prison. They found themselves in a tight place. What do you do when you find yourself in tight place, ready for release? The Bible declares that around midnight, they sang and prayed. These two powerful tools caused the prison doors to open and the loosening of chains. The jailer awakened from his sleep, saw the doors open and knew he lost his job, so he started to kill himself.

Paul said, "Do yourself no harm, we are still here." They waited to be released. They had an opportunity to walk out easily, but even the other prisoners waited. Not one of them escaped. What's the lesson here? Wait for God to release you into your purpose.

In the tight places (the cocoon of life,) your wings of flight develop for your ultimate release. Don't be deceived. All of us have tight places/cocoons. For example, the death of a loved one, financial difficulty, relational problems, health problems… Name your personal chrysalis. In these tight places, God is preparing you for your ultimate release.

For those of us awaiting God's time of release, the wait is over! It's flying time! Time to soar and release new ideas, new concepts, new communication. Creativity is about to spread its wings. This is your year to grow, spread your wings and fly.

For you have now been released to move about the country.

God did just that in my life, from 2012, the year of the divorce, to the present, He released me to minister to hundreds of hurting women, men, and children. He upgraded me to a luxury car that I was NOT looking for, increased my income, created Tonya Cunningham Ministries, added to the TCM Ministry team, and blessed me with a new power circle and uncommon favor!

If He did it for me, God will do it for you!

As I look back over my life, I see now that the times when I suffered the most were also the times I experienced the most spiritual and emotional growth. Because of my trials, I'm stronger, wiser, and better. I encourage you today to submit to your metamorphosis. It will help you grow, change, and learn how to live after loss.

Remember, there IS life after loss; it's just a different one! Soar my friend.

## Scripture: 2 Corinthians 5:17 NKJV

*"Therefore, if anyone is in Christ, he is a new creation; old things have passed away; behold, all things have become new."*

## Grief nugget:

"Just when the caterpillar thought the world was over, it became a butterfly."

~English Proverb

## Self-Reflection:

Are your wings still wet?

Are you willing to submit to your metamorphosis?

Have you fully embraced your new life?

# Bibliography

Dave Severson, G. B. (Producer), & Dave Severson, G. B. (Director). (2009-2012). *Hoarders* [Motion Picture]. Retrieved October 2015, from http://www.imdb.com/title/tt1497563/

Eddie Murphy, D. S. (Writer), & Landis, J. (Director). (1988). *Coming to America* [Motion Picture]. Retrieved October 18, 2015, from http://www.imdb.com/title/tt0094898/

Hawthorne, N. (1850). *The Scarlet Letter.* Boston, MA, USA: Ticknor & Fields. Retrieved October 2015

Jeff Arch, N. E. (Writer), & Ephron, N. (Director). (1993). *Sleepless in Seattle* [Motion Picture]. Retrieved October 10/18/2015, 2015, from http://www.imdb.com/title/tt0108160/

Kesey, K. (1962). *One Flew Over the Cuckoo's Nest.* New York, NY, USA: Signet.

Mayo Clinic Staff. (2014, May 08). *Diseases and Conditions-Hoarding Disorder.* Retrieved October 19, 2015, from Mayo Clinic: http://www.mayoclinic.org/diseases-conditions/hoarding-disorder/basics/definition/con-20031337

Michael Douglas, M. F. (Producer), & MilosForman (Director). (1975). *One Flew Over the Cuckoo's Nest* [Motion Picture]. USA. Retrieved October 15, 2015, from http://www.imdb.com/title/tt0073486/

United States Department of Labor. (2015, October 15). *Wage and Hour Division (WHD).* Retrieved from United States Deparment of Labor: www.dol.gov/whd/fmla/index.htm#forms

# ABOUT THE AUTHOR

Tonya is a visionary with over 25 years of professional experience in the funeral service/grief and loss industry.

In 2007, she launched her company as a Grief Facilitator and began grief support to groups for local funeral homes. Tonya quickly became known as "The Grief Lady" who helps people transition into their new life after a loss.

In 2013, she re-branded her company as Tonya Cunningham Ministries, which specializes in helping people heal holistically by providing practical tools to promote emotional, spiritual, and physical well-being.

By sharing her own story in book format, she hopes to help more people than she can reach physically find God's healing touch.

For more information about Tonya's ministry, or to contact the author, visit www.tonyacministries.com.

Made in the USA
Columbia, SC
28 September 2018